Praise for *The Brok*

Winner of the 2008 Cos

Winner of a Somerset Maugham Award

Shortlisted for the John Llewellyn Rhys Prize

"Dazzling . . . an exhilarating tour de force. Its thirty-three-year-old author moves around territory that is half a century and thousands of miles away from him with uncanny accomplishment. Place and period are conjured up as confidently as if he had been there. . . . What Foulds brings to the portrayal of violence and terror is the elegance of accuracy combined with emotional power and imaginative finesse. It makes his book—concise and precise, attentive and inventive—a superlative achievement."

—Peter Kemp, *The Sunday Times* (London)

"A miracle and a masterpiece."

—Sebastian Barry, author of *The Secret Scripture*

"Adam Foulds combines intricacy with momentum, line-by-line attentiveness with the first procedures of the storyteller, the lyrical with the epic. *The Broken Word* shows civilization breaking down in a nightmare of rape and murder, terror and tension. This alarming account of a forgotten colonial struggle tests people's capacity and marks a brilliant debut."

—Michael Longley

PENGUIN BOOKS

THE BROKEN WORD

Adam Foulds was born in 1974, took a Creative Writing MA at the University of East Anglia, and now lives in South London. His first novel, *The Truth About These Strange Times*, was published in 2007 and he was named *Sunday Times* Young Writer of the Year in 2008. His second novel, *The Quickening Maze*, which was shortlisted for the 2009 Man Booker Prize, was recently published by Penguin. *The Broken Word* was shortlisted for a number of awards, including the John Llewellyn Rhys Prize, and won the 2008 Costa Poetry Award.

THE BROKEN WORD

AN EPIC POEM OF THE BRITISH EMPIRE IN KENYA, AND THE MAU MAU UPRISING AGAINST IT

Adam Foulds

PENGUIN BOOKS

PENGUIN BOOKS

Published by the Penguin Group
Penguin Group (USA) Inc., 375 Hudson Street, New York, New York 10014, U.S.A.
Penguin Group (Canada), 90 Eglinton Avenue East, Suite 700, Toronto,
Ontario, Canada M4P 2Y3 (a division of Pearson Penguin Canada Inc.)
Penguin Books Ltd, 80 Strand, London WC2R 0RL, England
Penguin Ireland, 25 St Stephen's Green, Dublin 2, Ireland (a division of Penguin Books Ltd)
Penguin Group (Australia), 250 Camberwell Road, Camberwell,
Victoria 3124, Australia (a division of Pearson Australia Group Pty Ltd)
Penguin Books India Pvt Ltd, 11 Community Centre,
Panchsheel Park, New Delhi – 110 017, India
Penguin Group (NZ), 67 Apollo Drive, Rosedale, North Shore 0632,
New Zealand (a division of Pearson New Zealand Ltd)
Penguin Books (South Africa) (Pty) Ltd, 24 Sturdee Avenue,
Rosebank, Johannesburg 2196, South Africa

Penguin Books Ltd, Registered Offices:
80 Strand, London WC2R 0RL, England

First published in Great Britain by Jonathan Cape 2008
Published in Penguin Books 2011

1 3 5 7 9 10 8 6 4 2

Copyright © Adam Foulds, 2008, 2011
All rights reserved

ISBN 978-0-14-311809-1
CIP data available

Printed in the United States of America

THE BROKEN WORD

1: WHAT WAS HAPPENING

Compact glare of a match flame in daylight

and the waiter's dark hand still
as an ornament, the flame an upright leaf
tending to Jenkins as he sucked his cigarette alight,
because the train had slowed.
He wished it wouldn't slow, not
among the lion-coloured slums
with their cattery stink.
He could see people posting themselves,
third class, into the train windows or dropping
carefully onto wide, unfeeling feet.

The waiter waved out the flame.
Can I get you a drink, sir?
Sun's over the yard arm.

The waiter stood in the cylinder
of his white shift, understanding
or not. The train bucked,
gathering speed. He levelled himself
naturally as a glass of water.

Jenkins blew smoke towards him.

Also there is an Englishman, English boy,
sir, on the train with … other people.
Really? Who?
I don't know name, sir.
Well, tell him to come and see me,
and the answer is yes, bring me a drink.

*

The carriage dark with bodies.
Bright smells of opened fruit.
He asked questions and got
one old man talking because
he loved the plush impacts
of their consonants, the glimmer
of teeth, and had missed the sound
of thoughts fetched and weighed
and slowly spoken, ideas
that had formed slowly in the sun,
a million miles from the bark
and whine and snivel
and brag of school.
It soothed him. The noble cheekbones soothed him.

The old man looked like Joseph
from his own farm
who always had something
small and alive to show.
He spoke of his son in the city,
the difficult life, and ambition.

Then a cough, a touch on his shoulder.

Excuse me, sir. Mr Jenkins invites you
to go to him, please.

*

Tables. Empty Seats. Napery.
The proper way to sit.

This Jenkins, half-remembered, had a tweed moustache:
threads of ginger brown and white

I assume you don't smoke yet.

and hair so thin and waxed,
fastidiously flat,
it looked like a lick of paint.

You haven't been back long.
Jenkins observed the boy's white skin
as though the observation were cunning.

I flew in this morning.
And school?
Is finished. I go up to university in autumn.
Jenkins, who had not been, did not ask which one.
Final summer. You might have stayed in England,
you know. It might have been better.
Tom said nothing, then: *I wanted to come back.*

Jenkins held his cigarette down
into the ashtray until it was out,
the last smoke crawling up his hand, into his sleeve.

I presume your father has written to you
about the situation.

Tom, trying to pull his eyes politely
back from the view to Jenkins:
He mentioned it.

It's bad enough, Jenkins leaned forward
sending quiet words out one by one
like bees from the gap of their hive,
that you should not be in there
talking with them.

Tom blinked, fingertips on table edge.
But I've always . . .

Oh, we've all always but things are different.
The oathing has been going on
round your father's estate.

Oathing?

The ceremonies, the pledges:
join or your throat cut.
Or worse. Not far from here
two wouldn't.
Cut to bits, buried, dug up,
and then others forced to eat bits,
keep them in line. Of course
one broke down and spilled it.

Jenkins regarded Tom, the boy's
fingertips still on the table edge,
mouth slightly open, blushing
with fear, the fine and healthy fear
that might save him.

                                        *

Jenkins was met by Fuller
who led him to the car under trees already black,
the first stars prickling in their branches,
the two men walking, not talking.

Then, in the car, Fuller:
We've picked up two more.
Oh, yes?

4

Yes. Chaps got a bit worked up,
actually, sort of let them
have it somewhat.

*

Jenkins decided as soon as he saw
what a hash they'd made
of their faces, heard
their soft noises, lying there.

Mr Prior

the youngest there, smoking from
a flutter of fingertips, legs crossed,

            take these gentlemen
outside and end their suffering, would you.

Prior looked up. No one else looked.
When he had them up on their feet
and out of there, briefly,
at each other, they looked.

He made them walk in front.
Seeing their hands tied
in the smalls of their backs
his brain was smitten with a thought,
over-complicated, strictly meaningless,
like a fever thought:
the captives' captive hands
and he the captor. Three boxes: outermost he,
innermost their hands, their bodies'
own prisoners.
It made no sense.

Stepping with his dusty brogues
into the weak backs of their knees
he made them kneel
and to do it quicker than he could think
shot them   one   two
each opened head falling away
from his hand.

When Jenkins came out he looked up
and knew that there was more to do:
he'd have to clean
with bucket and sponge
each wet red gust
from the station wall.

                              *

Home. The door swings inward.
His father – not mother,
or servant, or sister –
his father, small eyes wet with joy,
it seemed, and then the shock
of the unaccustomed points
of his face against Tom's
for a second-long embrace,
then backing away, bowing,
Come in, come in.

6

Sipping the fragrant blue acid
of a gin and tonic
he watched the room deflate
behind his talking father.
Distended with imagining
when he came in
it became ordinary, actual, too quickly
while his father spoke too quickly
of cousins, small matters, prices.
His sister entered
carrying one of the cats.
She poured it out
onto heavy front paws
and an inconvenienced trot
to hold her brother lightly
by the shoulders and kiss –
mouth screwed up, the soft collision
of her cheekbone against his.

How are you, Kate?
Mm, she said, holding his gaze.
Where's Mum? She hiding?
She's out, Kate answered, *out in the fields.*
Mum is? His father crossed his legs.
Yes. Kate held his gaze.
I've bought a little telescope,
his father said, *for the stars. Like to see?*
Defo. In a minute. I must . . . refresh.
Right-oh.

A servant closed the door behind him; receded.
Tom stood a moment, half out
of focus with fatigue, and confused.
He walked towards the bathroom
and, passing, glanced into his father's study.
Books were piled; so now his father read.
He stepped in, heard his own voice,
as another cat, out of nowhere,
suddenly went.
He picked one up. Tennyson:
an old school prize.
Desk drawers were open.
And there was the new telescope
on its three legs, staring at the floor.
What was happening?
This, and the train. And there
was that old daub
in its place on the wall,
an eighteenth-century family thing,
a hunting scene,
its arrested motion like stopped clockwork
which had bothered him as a child,
birds stuck in a cream-cheese sky,
drab trees, reeds, grey water, curve
of a dog, the hunter trudging home
with his heavy bag.

2 : DINNER (1)

Frank was dead and he was very tired.

Frank was dead, dishevelled in his chair,
one ear falling away,
nose tip and lower lip gone,
dress shirt dyed plum.

Even through the thumps and flashes
of his own attack Charles had heard
with peculiarly greater concern
the *chit chit* of panga blades
into Frank's back
before the servants had retreated.

Frank was dead and Charles was exhausted.
He'd crawled up all the stairs,
the slow, successive risers,
gripping their tops,
pushing them down,
the last few almost too tall to scale,
to get to the shotgun under the bed.

It felt as if his fringe kept coming loose
but it was wide drips of blood
that fell everywhere. His hands
were syrupy with it,
also the two pieces of gun
that wouldn't shut together.
That catch . . . he couldn't:
it needed a fingertip that was gone.

He had a terrible headache.
Its massive pulse seemed outside
of him, one of them,
shaking the room.
Also the world had strangely blued,
with a wizening rim.

He swivelled in his leakage
and lay forwards
holding the two parts together
in a straight line towards the door.

3 : DINNER (2)

Kate in the bath before dinner.
Warm, soap-clouded water. Melodious drips.
Hair swaying heavily on her shoulders.

She sat up to look at her teeth
in the shaving mirror.
Two fingers in each side of her mouth,
lips jacked out and apart
to check for yellowness
of secret smoking.
She looked closely,
gasping and swallowing,
breathing through her nose, and saw
the smooth bevelled gums
flowing over the root of each tooth,
odd transparencies in the front teeth –
a sort of grain, near the bottom,
the colour of water –
the thick tongue that wouldn't lie still
behind its wall of teeth,
heavy and lifting, the edges curling,
dark blue veins and ugly strings beneath,
and, burning now with strain,
a link of skin between upper lip and gum
tight as a guy rope.
She dropped the lips back,
licked around, hummed
with everything back in place,
dabbled her finger ends in the bath.

*

A senior houseboy served the soup.
They skimmed their spoons correctly,
without noise, not touching china.

Leakey began again.
I should like to do it tomorrow,
if we can get them all together.

If you really think it's necessary.

It's a pointless risk if we don't.
Tom's mother was reasonable.

It is necessary, confirmed Jenkins.

Even if they haven't oathed themselves?

Done what? Kate asked.

Don't you ever read the papers?

Oathed themselves, Leakey repeated.

Tom looked at his large, calm, convincing head,
the gold cross perched slant on his collar-bone.
But a man who spoke Kikuyu better
than English, was almost one of them.
Then some of them were Christian too,
Tom reminded himself, the loyalists,
but not all of them. It was complicated.

Leakey set down his spoon before speaking,
an authority.

They swear freedom or death, an oath
that binds them together
to do whatever is decided.

Or death? So if they break it
they'll be killed, Tom reasoned.

Ah but the oath isn't properly binding,
just poor witchcraft.
These ceremonies can't be at night, for one thing.

Jenkins caught Tom looking at him.
It's a precaution, he said.

And what's in your ceremony?
Kate wanted to know.

Well, not all that they do.
We won't be sacrificing a goat
and drinking its blood, for instance.

They do that?

Ceremony leaves them insane.
Jenkins tore his roll. *Degenerates.*
They'll do anything. They drink
each other's blood as well. Tell them.

Sometimes, Leakey confirmed.
Incisions in the upper arms.
I don't think it's common.
They tell their god Ngai
to fight for them,
that he will be humiliated if they lose.
Their god. His God.
The two bars of gold,
dropped inside his shirt.
Leakey caught Tom's eye, smiled.
Have you ever drunk goats' blood?
You have to do it quickly

otherwise you're chewing down the clots.
Awful. Like . . . melting gristle.

Masai drink cows' blood, Tom pointed out.

We drink milk, Kate said.

Meaning what? her mother objected.

It's done under banana leaves,
my ceremony, which theirs always are.
And facing Ngai.
He dwells on Mount Kenya.
There's a special stone: the kisotho stone.

And blood pudding. And blood sausage.

Katy, do stop.

And Major Bloodnok.

Katy smirked with her father.

Leakey, swallowing soup,
eyelids lowered, submitted to smile.

Nurse, the screens!
Jenkins called to the servant by the door
who wavered forwards, was waved back.

So, Leakey spoke again,
how many are on your land?

Jenkins: *I hazarded a hundred,*
plus household staff.

I don't think we need worry about them.

Jenkins laughed, dabbing up soup.
I would start with them.

Tom's mother corrected.
It's a little less, nearer eighty.

And I hope you all know how to shoot.

Tom said, *I read this area was loyalist.*

Oh well then no doubt it's perfectly safe.
His father, loud and satirical.

What? Tom breathless, his face heating,
fed up of his father's snaps and ellipses.
Well, looking at his mother for support,
finding her face and Kate's
shut against the moment.
Well, isn't it?

But his father, head bent,
buttering three sides of a walnut-sized
tuft of bread, said nothing.

Jenkins answered.
*Oh, it is. We've been recruiting
for the Home Guard.
Military job, really,
but the Police Reserve, we've done
all sorts lately.
It hasn't been . . . entirely quiet.
And if they really turn . . .*

4 : FACING NGAI

Mid-morning after rain.
Mountains flowing rapidly under clouds.
The valley paths a freshened red
with yellow puddles, glittering weeds.

Tom walked between the lines
of coffee for half a mile,
knocking fragments
of water onto his sleeves –
little bubble lenses
that magnified the weave
then broke, darkening in.
He walked to within earshot
and no further.

A surprisingly dull sound of ceremony,
one voice then many voices,
one voice then many voices,
that recalled school chapel
although probably they were spared hymns.
Tom remembered the hymns,
the light, weakly coloured by the windows,
falling on the boys opposite,
standing, opening their mouths;
and the hymn books,
the recurrent pages greyish,
worn hollow like flagstones
with pressure of thumbs, over years,
years of terms, the books staying always
on their dark shelves in the pews.
The days he wanted to stay
all day alone in the pretty, scholarly chapel.

And then over the voices,
another sound.
Faintly, from behind the house,
Kate practising with a pistol,
its faint, dry thwacks
a fly butting against a window pane.

5 : NIGHT FIRES

Two bodies in the tree.

Home Guards touched them
with their torch beams,
feeling their way up
to the popped faces.
Two loyalist elders:
a headman and his brother.
Someone found where one rope
was tied to the trunk
and hacked through.
The headman dropped vertically
onto his heels, bounced, landed
again, sank sideways, staring.

Careful. Please.

Sir, do you hear something?

The sergeant, realising:
Who told us to come here?
Who told us this was here?

*

The patrol pulled into the sergeant's own village
to see it almost finished. No one screaming.
The men labouring hard, quietly, as in a workshop,
a boat builders' yard,
limbs and parts scattered around them,
their wet blades in the flamelight
glimmering rose and peach.

The wheezing collapse of a burning hut,
its final volley of sparks, inches long,
snapping through greasy blackness, into nothing.

The sergeant emptied his revolver,
spun one man onto the ground.
The others flashed like fish and disappeared.

After them!

*

Tom sat for the first time
on the glimpsed adult furniture
of the gentlemen's bar
of the East Highlands Country Club.
Creaking maturity of wood and leather.
Marine, meditative drifts of cigar smoke
wandering around him. He hurried
its blue curves with his own breath
while the men talked.

                    And the men talked.
Tom's accession could hardly distract them.
His father's introductions
grew more buttonholing, hucksterish.

Talk was of Frank Grayson and Charles Hewitt,
the two old boys who dined together,
clobbered by their own servants,
just absolutely butchered.
And there were other incidents –
everyone had something from his own farm.
And the Governor was *no more use*
than a margarine dildo.

Tom had had a nightmare the previous night:
he and Kate in the corridor
down to matron's room,
building a barricade of chairs,
permeable, collapsing, clatteringly rebuilt,
which wouldn't keep anybody out.
Aside from that, he'd found it hard to fear
consistently. At home he kept forgetting.
Everything looked so much as always,
the objects placid, the weather, the days like others.
Here among these men who'd simmered
for weeks in their adrenalin,
his own fear took shape, hardened,
with edges, between his lungs.

No one really spoke to him.
Prior of the KPR was there
and closest to Tom's age
but he spoke to no one,
or nodded at what Jenkins said.

In the panelled room
the men's tans looked wrong.
Nervy, thickening, strained,
their faces looked dirtied by the sun.
Unsettled: they'd thought their major war over.
Sitting by Tom's father, Monty Parker's
face had a cracked glaze,
white crows' feet showing through.
One of the old set,
his vigorous enterprise
with other men's wives might not
have surprised Tom if he'd been told.
He remembered him jogging
round a pool in dripping trunks,
smiling out to his incisors,
instigating games.

You bunking up here tonight?

Tom answered, his father watching:
We weren't planning on it.

Monty leaned back, slid
his palms down his chest.
I suppose it's not too far for you.
I will. MMBA for me to get back.
Then unpacked the familiar slang
with leisured loathing:
Miles and miles of bloody Africa.

A message for Jenkins pulled him from the room.
It looked urgent.
Trouble in the nursery
got no laughs.

When he returned, he was followed
by a Home Guard Johnny
who loitered by the door
unaware of his audacity,
breathing hard, in a filthy uniform,
shoes splashed, Tom noticed, and not with mud.

Jenkins stood in the middle of the room.
Gentlemen, there's a hunt on.
There's been a ferocious carve-up,
maybe a hundred loyalists are dead.
The Mau Mau are out there
in their villages right now, or hiding.
Would you all care to join me
in going after these fucking apes.
There are guns for everybody.

Monty Parker stood up, clapped.
Right. I want to bag me a brace
of these awful niggers.

Prior stood up,
checking his pockets.

Tom's eyes met his father's.
I ought to go back,
for Kate and your mother.
Can't leave them undefended
with this going on.

Of course.

But you should go, Tom.
You'll be useful. And it's time,
I'm afraid, you know,
to be a man and all that.

Jenkins was beside them: *Well?*

Get one for me, Tom.
So Tom's father offered Tom,
offered him up
with an awkward shove
as men offer their sons
out into the world.

I'm heading back to ours.
My wife and daughter.
Tom's all for it, though.

Good, good. Prior will sort you out.

*

Equipped, going, in an open–
backed vehicle, with torch and gun
and whistle, gripping the metal frame
as stars tossed and righted themselves,
the vehicle flounced and skittered
down the terrible road,
Tom felt awfully close to laughing.
His chest seethed with it.
All these men, armed,
some still in their bow-ties,
grave-faced, could they mean it?
The whole thing was ludicrous:
the boy-scout planning, the boxes of ammo.
Prior sat forwards, holding the muzzle

of his rifle with both hands,
riding easily, without seeming to notice
the sudden wincing drops and sickening floats.

Out of the vehicles. Into the stillness
of a night of loud insects.
Cooling engines ticked.
Hysteria subsided: they *were* serious.
And the night's soft, huge darkness approached,
breathed up behind them,
shaping for murder. Tom felt it touch
the back of his head. In the twisting
torch lights they made decisions.
Tom was assigned to two Home Guards
whose names he didn't catch
and his throat closed when he tried to ask,
his inner surfaces clamping.
They would roam for hideaways
away from the villages.
Others would start at the villages
and clean them out.

*

Began for Tom a difficult walk.
He felt weightless with fear
but hurt with effort – these men
walked fast – and black shapes
sometimes hit him, branches.
He felt, he really felt,
the trajectory from the end of his gun,
a line, a beam, projecting
hundreds of yards, loose,
swinging as he walked,
slicing through, and all along
that line whenever he wanted it, death.

Prior saw her, the pretty cropped head,
the high breasts, the wide frightened eyes,
and grabbed her by the forearm,
the decision made in his body
before he had thought:
to leave the men and their business,
to grab and vanish with her.
He pulled her arm, starting to run.
Quick, girl. Very dangerous here.
Come on. Safer. Safer!

*

Everything flocking into darkness.
Tom had to keep after them to see.
Glimpses flared, were lost,
kept plunging out of sight,
if they were glimpses.
His weightless legs bumped under him,
cringed at distant gunfire.
His two men stopped.
There, pointing at the richer, feathered black of undergrowth.
When I say. Tom raised his gun.
Now. And all fired.
Tom saw his extended arm in flashes
as the shots went off.
A voice in his head counted the bangs,
totalled seven between them.
Cease fire! They walked to the spot.
One Home Guard nudged the body with his foot.
Tom looked, then up at the lurching trees.
It had looked just like a man.
The way the fingers curled.

You got your first, sir.
Tom tucked his hot gun
into his waistband to be able
to shake their hands.

*

The place Prior found was so dark
that he could hardly see her:
a flex of mauve on her skin,
the white corners of her eyes.
Certainly no one would hear them,
much less care, what with the shrieks and gunfire.
She gave him no trouble to speak of.
After one good slap that salted her mouth
she was compliant, only
repeating some phrase over
and over, like a bird's stupid song.
But he was right, he was right
to take her. Face down,
with a little forcing – her phrase getting faster –
he was in, pushing, pushing,
her buttocks greasy, cold against his belly,
her little breaths shunted out
in time to him, her warm, elegant
neck in his right hand,
her left bicep in his left,
her dry hole burning him.
Breezes lifted the sweat from him.
After his narrow, painful release,
No harm done. Good girl,
he lit a cigarette then helped her up
and, smoking, watched her run away.

*

Why had Tom thought they'd stop
after the first kill, as though they'd done enough?
Of course they didn't.
Over the long night they killed two more,
a modest tally by others' standards.
The second one Tom didn't shoot.
He held his gun up while the others shot
and watched him fall.
The third came after long hours,
with splintery light through the trees.
By now, trekking back,
they could smell the burning villages everywhere.
Tom's legs itched horribly.
His shirt sucked at his skin,
rubbed a slow burn into his collar.
There were bodies everywhere
in different attitudes:
stunned, reaching, sleeping, tumbled.
Then from behind something a man sprang up
and Tom shot him.
Just like in a Western: the attacking Indian:
Tom saw the man look straight at him,
clownish with terror
as he pulled the trigger,
saw the bullet make a splash
in the man's bare chest.
Only the fall backwards was different,
looser and ugly, spastic, almost embarrassing.
A Home Guard walked up sideways,
slowly, and shot again the wriggling man.

*

Back at the vehicles, the men murmured,
passing round a hip-flask.
The sky was oppressively bright,
acres of weightless gold above them.
Prior saw Tom's face
and walked over to him,
placed his hand on Tom's shoulder.
You'll be all right, old man.
Chipper after some sleep.
First time is always the worst.
Tom turned, unable . . . to thank,
and held on to his wrist.

6: SCREENING

Truck after truck from the cleared cities,
ordered off the back, marshalled,
bullied into line, then ordered
past Tom and his rifle on the way in,
and each of them as they passed
glanced up at him, into him,
all their eyes the same colour.
It made Tom think, in detail,
of the famous Chinese water torture,
the drop drop drop on the top of your head
until the skin breaks,
the drops are deafening,
pain tunnels down, blooms
into the brain's furthest corners,
drowning everything.
Each glance louder in his head.

He waved them onward with his gun

to a table of his superiors
and their informants,
men (or women) hidden in plain sight
in hoods down to their feet.
As they filed past, the hoods
dipped like blown candle flames, deciding.

*

Tom learned to prefer fence patrol
for the solitude, walking counter-clockwise,
every twelve minutes
passing his fellow walking clockwise.

So he could pace out the hours
awaiting assignment
to a permanent camp
and tire himself before bed.

Noises from that hut. He walked over, listened, entered.
A prisoner on a table. Men around him.
A pistol. Lit cigarettes. The men intent.
The viscous, adult atmosphere
of a poker game. The prisoner's eyes,
as they slowly turned to find Tom,
like something sliding down a wall.

One of the men:
*You can join in the fun
or keep strolling. What d'you fancy?*

Tom, when he could, apologised, closed the door.

Outside the sun was just down and the horizon,
past distant burnt-out tree shapes, was black.
The air was clear. The sky looked scientific,
a clear demonstration, its arch
grading through unseeable fractions of colour
from damp eye-blue to the wide western red.
He breathed.
He paced the fence,
resting his hands on his rifle.

Two shots from the hut.
A smattering of applause
as from a cricket pavilion.

Pushed down with his wrists
until the strap burned one side of his neck.

Passing the other patrol.
Buck up, old thing. Who pissed
in your rice pudding?

Loudly: *What do you want, a bloody tap dance?*

Then from the watch tower, making Tom jump:
Ladies, ladies. Please.
I am a-trying to run a respectable hestablishment.

Jesus, fucking prats. Tom walked off.

A hundred yards of wire, diamonds of sky.
The night getting colder, whirring,
fur-trimmed with moths.
Tom walking it out of his system,
passing the other patrol without
saying anything, walking and walking

and then a noise ceasing at the fence.
Tom walked towards it and saw
legs, long-soled feet.
As he grew close, they started moving again
like frantic clockwork, pushing,
the man's back raked by the wire.
Tom grabbed the ankles and pulled.
Going somewhere? Going to leave us all behind?
In his rage, he forgot his training
and beat him
not with the butt but the barrel of his gun.
He swung and swung
across the breaking stave
of the man's forearms and collar bone
until it seemed the prisoner shivered
and gradually fell asleep,
but Tom, Tom had too much energy and carried on.

7: COMPOUND NINE

Tom overseeing the Home Guard
overseeing bucket fatigue.
Four men crouched with the latrine buckets
on their heads, running as flat as possible,
skimming their burning feet, but splashed
at each turn. Running until they fell.
Tom almost couldn't bear
the flashing of galvanised metal.
He turned, snorted, and spat effectively,
a glistening single bolt of inner yellow
that stood erect on the dirt.

He didn't feel good.
Maybe he was ill. It was hard to tell.
The heat up north was dreadful
and he sweated all day, from his scalp down.
Gritty, dragging wetness.
An endless revolting birth.

Diseases among the prisoners
brought the quieter, night-time deaths,
but Tom was well-fed, inoculated.
Maybe just a cold or flu.
He wiped his forehead
with the dusty back of his hand, raised it
in feeble excuse and walked away.

Gun-belt off, boots off, back on his cot,
the damp pillow that smelt of his head.
He reached out and touched the wooden wall behind.
Rubbed with his palm it made a husky sound.
Good dog, he said. *Good dog.*

He woke with a start, wet-faced,
the corners of his eyes smarting from his own salt
but an arid clearness high in his nose,
a sense of lengthened tunnels up
into his forehead. He shifted
and a letter slid off of his chest.
So something had woken him.
He looked: Baxter was delivering post.
Baxter smiled, spoke cod-Irish for some reason:
'Tis news from the old country, to be sure.
It was: the Queen's pretty Victorian silhouette
under an English postmark.
He checked the back: Kate.

Dear Scruffbag. Hope you're well and all that.
How's life as a man of action? A constant source
of astonishment to you, I should think.
You didn't tell me much
about it in your epistle. Is it all very Dornford Yates
and super hush-hush? As for me,
I'm perfectly safe and bored, bored, bored.

She'd looked up from her first three lines
at the rain-thickened kitchen window,
the blue daisy of gas flame under the soup.

His eye skimmed down: news about an aunt,
a pet bird going bald, a girl he didn't remember
but who remembered him, and then

33

Did I ever tell you what mummy
told me about daddy in the war?
I thought it might explain things a little.
I don't remember the details but
something about hearing a man
trapped inside a tank that was on fire.
Apparently daddy had a stammer
for a few months! Awful.
Anyway, scruffbag, be heroic
and you'll be famous:
it's in all the papers over here,
with pinkos protesting and the like.

He folded the pages back into the envelope,
dropped it into his bedside drawer.
He thought about the pet bird
becoming poultry with its patches
of pimpled bare skin, and
pouring a kettle of boiling water
directly onto them.

*

Another morning. Sunlight steepening.
The prisoners cross-legged, being counted,
then staring forward but ordered to watch.
Tom watched for a bit. He'd grown a connoisseur
of beatings: the first blows stunning and accurate,
with feints or not, and large, like sculpture.
But quickly the prisoner couldn't focus,
looked ridiculous, bewildered, lonely
before they blacked out completely and lay there.

*

(The black flies, soft as hair
as they landed on you,
shivered half an inch
in any direction, bristly bodies throbbing,
before setting down the delicate leg
of their mouthparts, and the smaller,
hard-bodied flies that glittered like ordnance
and fizzed around the buckets.
Rapid, unconscious, blameless.

The flies landed on you
and you waved them off, they
curved around your hand
like water and landed again
to sip at tear fluid and saliva,
to eat the dead skin, dirt, lay their eggs
in the nutritious wetness of wounds.

There was no way to get rid of them,
you just waved at their persistence
for hours, until you fell asleep.)

At least pay attention. At least look.

*

Tom sat at his place at one
of the English tables in the mess,
eating beef in gravy, tightening the vice
of his molars until the meat's
staunch fibres gave way.
Opposite him, Johnson, until recently
a recent settler, over from Surrey,
already on his sponge pudding,
making sure that each spoonful
wore a thick sneer of custard.

Safe inside a reputation
for hardly talking to anyone,
Tom rested his forehead on his fingers, chewed,
stared down at his swimmy brown plate,
and listened to the faint, forthright tick
of his watch by his left ear.

Chaps, just so you know what's happening

Tom looked up: Compound Eleven's senior officer.
Ornate ears, a burnt nose, his hair
somehow endearingly combed,
Tom rather liked him.
He seemed just to want things done.
His motor always turning over,
one leg joggling under the table.

I'll do a formal run-down later
but gist is a letter has been found.
To that bloody Castle woman.
Now I think we'd better come down hard,
send a few of them over
to the specialists in Compound Nine.
We'll muster them early.

He breezed out. The Home Guard
at their table almost bowed.

*

Tom shivered in the early sweat-drying sun.
In its slant light
the prisoners heads smouldered,
their hair reddish and fluffy
with kwashiorkor. Tom blinked
at ninety-four dying men
and half of them in clown-wigs
cross-legged on the floor, listening to the voice.

. . . letters passed under the fence
to go out with the work gangs . . .

Running his fingertips across
the rash inside his collar,
the warm, uneven skin.

The following prisoners are to be sent
to Compound Nine for further interrogation.
Stand up when your number is called.
Prisoner 1435. Prisoner 2822.

They unfolded their legs and stood,
so thin their knees looked big
as pulley blocks. Home Guard
strode across to tie their wrists.

Prisoner 4116. Prisoner 1607.

Prisoner 1607 began to moan
and tipped over, writhing in the dust.
(Another phrase Tom had learned
the meaning of in the camp. Writhing
in the dust. He'd watched men do it.)
Home Guard rushed over to lift him
but he poured himself down
over and over through their hands,
moaning, lolling his head,
all his muscles refusing. When he was struck
his face cleared. His mouth set
with the angry assurance of the mad.
He shouted: *I give up the oath.*
Please. Please. I give up the oath.
I am not Mau Mau, not rebel. Please.

And so his war ended.
He was taken aside to go through the forms
and then released to find
whatever remained of his village.

So few broke the oath these days
that Johnson winked triumphantly at Tom.
Those who would break had gone
in the first months. The remaining
men would rather die,
their oaths preserved like crystals
somewhere inside their broken bodies.
But why? Tom didn't understand.
Why not just lie to get out
then carry on? Witchcraft, maybe. Leakey would know.

Two more numbers were called.
The five were led out,
past three prisoners up to their necks
in the ground for a minor offence,
their heads sticking up like croquet hoops.

*

Three weeks later two of the men came back,
wordless and unsteady, heavily edited. Between them:
nine fingers, two ears, three eyes, no testicles.
No good to anyone, they were let out
to wander briefly as mayflies
and die as a warning.

*

Arm high over his head, he flexed
his little black leather bible
like a muscle sprung from his body.
His centre-parted hair flapped
its stumpy wings as he jerked,
his pale lips gymnastic.

*Because God's forgiveness is total,
Christ's love unconditional,
His grace here and now is available to you
if you would but open your hard hearts to him.
For he rejoiceth in the sinner*

Denominations on a rota.
Today: The Church of Scotland.
He shrieked and pointed and quoted
and then sounded very calm and reasonable.
At least it wasn't the Catholic, Father O'Brien,
who last time had pulled one round by his hair
and kicked him onto his knees.

Pour out my heart like water before the Lord.
Evidently he meant it. The man
was almost crying.
The Christian prisoners crossed themselves
and said *Amen* at the ends of prayers
but nothing else. He preached
his heart out in the sun.

*

Days.

The sun detonating
its hydrogen.

Sores growing on the prisoners like coral.

Buckets. Drills. Beatings. Boredom.

Tom retaining ever less of himself.
He'd seen a hide prepared once on the farm,
the creamy, yellowish fat of the underside
corrugating in front of the strigil
then deftly slapped into a wooden bowl
for some other purpose.
The scraped hide, hung up after, kicking in the wind.

Sleep each night like falling into a well.
Rats and slime. Each morning,
the long climb back up
to where the others were waiting.

*

Right bunch o' naughty bastards for you.

Lancashire Fusiliers with a lorry of new arrivals.

From the forests. Bugger to catch, they were.
We collected hands before, as tally,
but General Bobby blew a gasket.

The sun had burned through the soldier's cheeks.
Under flaking brown paper, cold pink marble.

So they're your look-out now.

Cummings, who was thickly muscled
and never wore a shirt,
hassled and slapped them into line,
disposed of an awkward one immediately,
with a little playground shove
into the outer ditch of stakes.

Oopsy-daisy.

Inside, they stripped at gunpoint.
Famished but strong. Their bones
strapped together with long muscles.
Tom admired them.

He'd hiked once in the forests,
with his father. And only once.
The ground was steep, up the foothills.
So dense, with the sense of something seething
just out of sight. Circling venoms. Biting insects.
And the streams when you reached them
shrieked down from the heights,
freezing in the narrow channels.

He stayed to watch them beaten and clothed.
One of them, the tallest, although
his penis shrivelled with fear,
stayed standing longer than anyone he'd seen.

*

The guards didn't like them.
They spoke too much at night.
They were a new element.
There was a hardening in the stares
of the other prisoners.

Father O'Brien was unleashed against them
for an afternoon demonstration
of an eternity in hell.

Nothing.

Tom loved to see them withstand their punishment,
their heads whipped around
like wildflowers in a breeze.

Johnson tried to hack at their morale.
General China's already working for us.
You know that, don't you?
You're about the last lot to be caught.
So what's the point in carrying on.
Kimathi will give in the same way,
once he's run out of bum-boys in the woods.
He'll be working for Her Majesty by Christmas.

And then the tall man raised a finger and answered.

Shut up! The Home Guard.

What's he saying?

Shut up!

He translated, himself, into English:
I'm saying you do not know Kimathi.
He cannot be caught.

Shut up!

When you try to catch him,
he can become a bird.

Yes. Tom whispered to himself.

He can become a snake.
He can become wind in the sky.

Yes. Yes.

Shut up!

Or one drop of water
to hide in the stream.
So how can this man be catched?

Right. The commander, hands raised, shaking his head
like a dissatisfied choirmaster.
This one's just bought a ticket to Compound Nine.

Oh, no he hasn't, Tom whispered.

A Home Guard pulled him to his feet
and Tom quickly drew his pistol.
Like slapping a toy from his hands,
he shot him through the head.
The wetted Home Guard, mouth open,
terrified, checked from side to side.
He looked like a startled dog.

Sorry, Tom laughed, raising his hand,
waving his gun. *I'm sorry*.

Home. The door swings inward.
A servant, his face relaxing
with recognition, then his mother
drifting into the vestibule.

Tom. You didn't say you were coming.

But here I am.

Yes, you are, aren't you.
She rubbed his left upper arm,
chewing her smile.

*

The familiar food, the furniture –
the way the armchair by his window
spread behind his shoulder blades
and supported his thighs.
Tom could have cried.

*

Eventually:

I'm just a little concerned, Tom.
His mother, pouring tea
into three cups. His father
tightening in his chair.
About you just giving up like this.

Actually, that isn't quite what happened.

His father broke a biscuit,
shook crumbs from the two halves.
It's not really a habit you should acquire.

Tom, don't sigh like that.

I didn't sigh. His voice was loud.
They riled him so easily.
He sipped tea, felt it rush
around his teeth, and recommenced
with a lawyerly, factual, frangible calm.
I didn't just give up.

*Have you thought about this being just
a little holiday here and then going back?*

Back? He looked up,
then down, falling back in his seat,
mouth slowly closing.
They watched him closely,
thought he hated the idea
but his actual thought was:
It *is* still there. They're all still there,
save for the newly dead.
No. No. I want to start next term.

I mean to say, aren't you needed?

What he could tell them about there,
if he wanted, to shut them up.
If they believed him.
But it wasn't even possible,
so wildly unmentionable,
like bringing up wet dreams
or school things.
Impossible.
I told you, it was agreed.

His father tried to sting him
into it. *Well, you're a man now.*
You can make your own decisions.

But it was a weak lunge
and after it, they were all still there,
waiting, and it was Tom, in fact, deciding.
It made him think
Who are these people?
The frightened man with his telescope
and strapping, sunburnt wife?

Yes, I am. Yes, I am.
And I reckon I've done my bit.

He took a biscuit
almost not trembling.
But his mother was effective.
Tom, I don't want you living
with the shame of crying off
of something difficult for the rest of your life.

Tom put down his biscuit, finished his tea,
and threw the cup against the wall.
It smashed wonderfully, as though charged,
into a thousand tiny white knives and powder.
Tom looked over the whole service,
deaf with pleasure, considering them for bombs.

9: RAIN

Rain strafing the river.

Tom under the ringing bell
of an oak, his face and hands
glazed with the cold damp.
One drop, falling through, landed
amusingly on his parting.

Deep plashing green, the lavish
sound of water drenching water,
rain thickening to whiteness in gusts.
And the large calm of changeable weather:
passing showers, thinking skies.
Tom silent, having to wait.

*

The large, composed silence of the library
with its little human lapses: coughs,
rustled paper, the bump of books.
Thrumming a card index, the corners
of popular titles soft as seed heads
where the glue had worn away,
the fibres coming loose.

Then back at his carrel
contentedly at work
with the Meccano
of an ancient grammar.

Bright metalwork of Trojans, Danaans,
well-greaved Achaeans
buckling and unbuckling
over an abstract plane
as he went over and over,
adjusting his translation.

*

Tom picked up his tutor's small coal shovel
and beat his blotchy head.
The tutor fended with vague, slender hands,
What on earth are you doing?
leaking dinges in his skull,
eyes clouding, Tom athletically
rendering him down until
the whole study was lacquered red,
chair, lamp shades, pictures, books, and Tom himself,
that old penny taste of blood in his mouth.

He wiped his face on his pillow,
considering the variations
in this version of the dream,
then got up to be gone
before his scout came in.
Better to go out altogether
and avoid college breakfast.
Instead he went to a café
where he could sit, eat eggs
and foam-flecked rashers
and feel like an open sewer,
deep poison seeping from him,
and not be seen by anyone he knew.

*

Freedom. Solitude. Rain.
Infusions of books. Girls close by.
Everything hidden. The people gentle,
about their business, unprovoked.
Shortening days, like a coat pulled tighter.

10: FALLING ASLEEP

Spring. The river besotted with light.

On the path a small shadow
pulsed with the breeze, slid
back and forth over the toe of his shoe.

He rolled an ant from his page,
its glittery black body sticky
as a candied fruit. It left
just the faintest strawberry taint
over the page with Tom's marginal gloss:

swim

summer's	*dark cloud*
liquid air	*down wind*
admire/	
observe	

leafy shelter

*

He'd seen her before at lectures
and sat now deliberately behind her
to look down onto her tender nape,
the blue thread of ink from her fountain pen
she tied into beautiful knots.
When she turned her head slightly
he could see the frill of eyelashes
settling on the curve of her cheek.
Dark brown hair. Neat hands.

Outside, he lengthened his stride after her,
past, he was sure, two other chaps closing in,
and, refusing to listen to his brain,
said grossly, out of nowhere: *Hello.*

She turned; smiled. *Hello.*

*That was . . . did you . . . that was
a little dull.* Which he didn't
actually think and regretted
when she answered patiently, *I suppose.*

He was rubbing his forehead for some reason.
*Listen, do you have time, we could
. . . have time for tea?*

She looked at her wrist, so white and small,
and laughed. *I haven't got my watch on.*

*

Dining in hall: a recession of tables,
lamplit. Swift, soft-footed service.
What was wrong? Something. Conversations
definitely about him curved out of earshot.
He felt open, air touching him, and discovered
that his arse was bare, and raw.
Despicable public meat he couldn't cover.

*

He couldn't picture her face not smiling.
There was always at least
the glimmering start of a smile,
her lips closed, dimples deepening.
That deranged him with pleasure.
Anything could be funny with her
which kept them always airborne
and full of fluttery secrets. Single words
could trigger them off.
They made light of childhoods and homes
and everyone around them. Made light.
Tom made light of his military career.

*

For their first evening date
he bought tickets to a concert
and walked her there.
Solemnly happy, neither had anything to say.
Tom listened to the knock
of his good shoes on the pavement,
the sharp report of heels
that made her taller,
slower, a definite woman.

A whitewashed space like a church.
The luminous fade of evening
against clerestory windows.
Eleanor beside him, small again,
compact and intelligent.
He thought of leaning his thigh against hers
but she sat quite separately,
her feet, hooked at the ankles, swinging
to a stop under her seat.

Her hand claps like flapping cloth
when the quartet walked on
because of the gloves she wore.

He leaned into the prickling air around her,
close enough to smell her smell.
The players rocked on their chairs,
patent shoes creaking, their elbows pistoning
in complex staggered agreement.

Not especially musical, Tom watched
their faces go blank with concentration
or smile for a phrase, or, purse-mouthed,
strenuously meet each other's gaze
to establish a difficult convergence.

Outside, feeling suave: *Shall we walk?*

You can walk me back to college,
it's not long till curfew.

Certainly. That was nice.

Yes. Lovely.

Blue clouds and stars between towers.
Small trees, like penned animals, behind walls.
Eleanor allowed Tom her arm
which he held very carefully
as though he might snap the bone,
and tried to feel, to listen along it,
to feel deeper into her body.

Eleanor was the first of them to understand
that a commotion further up the street
was two men fighting outside a pub.

Good Lord, ought we to do something?

Tom looked at them, staggering,
pushing each other's heads
with slovenly round-armed punches,
not even a drop of blood,
all their insides inside.
They're not hurting each other.

But they're punching each other.

Light-headed, made fond
by her ignorant concern,
he started to boast.
If you want to see them hurt,
I know how to make them suffer.

What?

I . . . I mean . . . his breath was short.
All over his body, blue-black: crow feathers.
What? He muttered something normal
or inaudible
then someone came out of the pub,
Hey, hey, hey, boys
and pulled them apart.

He left her at a decent distance
from her college gates.
Well, good night, then.
Yes, good night.
That was lovely, I mean
worth doing again.

Oh, certainly, she smiled. *Very worthwhile.*
He bent forwards to kiss her cheek,
lacking courage, then finding it and swerving
so that he kissed cool skin
and the lively wriggle of the corner of her lips.
Good night.
He held her waist and pulled her
so the front of her body met his,
kissed directly her mouth.
Lummy. Naughty, she smiled. *Good night –*
I think I've said that.
Tom grinned, *I think you did.*

She waved before she disappeared
in through the little door.
Tom clapped once, silently cheered,
then limped home smiling,
his anguish in his pocket.

*

Lying beside one another on the grass,
inspecting faces, trying not to laugh.
Tom noticed the delicate fizz of light
along her jaw like a nettle stem.
In the inner corners of her eyes,
tiny submerged pink – what? – like
cushions or pleats, and beside them

in the whites' gathering convexity,
beneath bending tree reflections,
the finest threads of blood.
What? What have you found?
Everything jumping.
Sshh, I can't concentrate.
In her throat, a half-inch
of artery that pulsed.
Hmm. Little larva.
Touching it with a fingertip.
A half-pumped inner tube,
but alive. For a moment
he saw her whole head scarlet
and glistening, her teeth
folding back under a good thick stick.
God, he said out loud.
What?
Nothing. Lie still.
To put it out of his head,
he leaned over and kissed her
hard, pushing down to find
the moment of consent
and introduced his tongue.
He felt her eyes open
and close again as she responded
with a strong, blunt prod
of her own tongue back at his.
Wonderful. The time was right.
He took hold of her left breast
through her clothes, and squeezed,
still kissing, taking his time.
Then he slid his hand down
to the bottom of her skirt
and stroked the bony hump of her knee.
Then moving on again,

58

onto the smoothness of thigh
and up, short of breath,
getting as far as her underwear,
the disquieting, burnt grass
dry crackle of hair
through the cloth, flesh
beneath it, before she'd had
enough and grabbed his wrist.
He kept his hand there,
using his strength. She
disengaged her mouth.
Tom. Please be nice.
I am being nice.
Pushing against her lovely weakness,
pressing the warm cloth up into her gap.
Tom. Don't. Please, now.
But why not?
She kicked herself upright,
retied her hair.
I have to go anyway.
No, you don't.
I think I know whether I do or not. Bye.

*

Days. Bad nights.

He wrote her a letter
full of wrangling and declaration,
the dreadful phrases afterwards
circling in his mind like bits
of dirty paper in the flush.

And then the thought of when she really
knew him – he should just give up.

After that he saw her in the street
talking with a friend, presumably
the Elizabeth she'd mentioned.
Well the bitch must know
all about him by now.
Eleanor saw him and, still talking,
took one step with her left leg,
rounding her shoulder to keep him out.

Lack of sleep had him running
a mild fever, his skin papery,
eyesight thick, joints achy.
The silence of libraries
a hissing sea-sound that sent him
into the briefest sleeps,
head falling, jaw gone cretin-slack.
Ridiculous: he was there, he was away,
but she'd made it not enough.

When he saw her again
the street slurred around him,
his peripheral vision smeared
with passing gowns, swish cars,
and herself in the centre,
arms folded, unsmiling,
waiting for what he would say.
Really he was almost too tired
to talk. *I'm sorry, about the other day.*
Hrrr. I'm, ah, sorry . . .
What could he say, mouth dry,
and everything he'd done?
Just wanting to climb inside her,
to crawl into the darkness
of her body and fall asleep.

But then she spoke. *Tom.*
His name in her voice,
softening through him.
Tom, I was hoping I'd see you.

Yes?

Yes. I think, she smiled, *well,*
I've been missing you.

Really?

You sound surprised. Look,
it's just, well, if you want
things to . . . progress, usually
young men start looking,
you know, do I have to
spell it out? In jewellers' windows.

ACKNOWLEDGMENTS

This poem was published in two parts in *Areté* magazine, issues 20 and 22.

I am deeply indebted to Craig Raine and Adam Frost for advice and encouragement.